What in the World Is a Violin?

Mary Elizabeth Salzmann

Consulting Editor, Diane Craig, M.A./Reading Specialist

A Division of ABDO

ABDO
Publishing Company

visit us at www.abdopublishing.com

Published by ABDO Publishing Company, a division of ABDO, P.O. Box 398166, Minneapolis, Minnesota 55439. Copyright © 2012 by Abdo Consulting Group, Inc. International copyrights reserved in all countries. No part of this book may be reproduced in any form without written permission from the publisher. Super SandCastle™ is a trademark and logo of ABDO Publishing Company.

Printed in the United States of America, North Mankato, Minnesota
092011
012012

 PRINTED ON RECYCLED PAPER

Editor: Elissa Mann
Content Developer: Nancy Tuminelly
Cover and Interior Design: Colleen Dolphin, Mighty Media, Inc.
Photo Credits: Shutterstock, Thinkstock

Library of Congress Cataloging-in-Publication Data

Salzmann, Mary Elizabeth, 1968-

 What in the world is a violin? / Mary Elizabeth Salzmann.

   p. cm. -- (Musical instruments)

 ISBN 978-1-61783-208-6

 1. Violin--Juvenile literature. I. Title.

 ML800.S26 2012

 787.2'19--dc23

                    2011023171

Super SandCastle™ books are created by a team of professional educators, reading specialists, and content developers around five essential components—phonemic awareness, phonics, vocabulary, text comprehension, and fluency—to assist young readers as they develop reading skills and strategies and increase their general knowledge. All books are written, reviewed, and leveled for guided reading, early reading intervention, and Accelerated Reader® programs for use in shared, guided, and independent reading and writing activities to support a balanced approach to literacy instruction.

Contents

What Is a

A violin is a musical instrument.

Violin?

The **main** parts of a violin are the tuning pegs, the neck, the strings, the body, the bridge, and the chin rest.

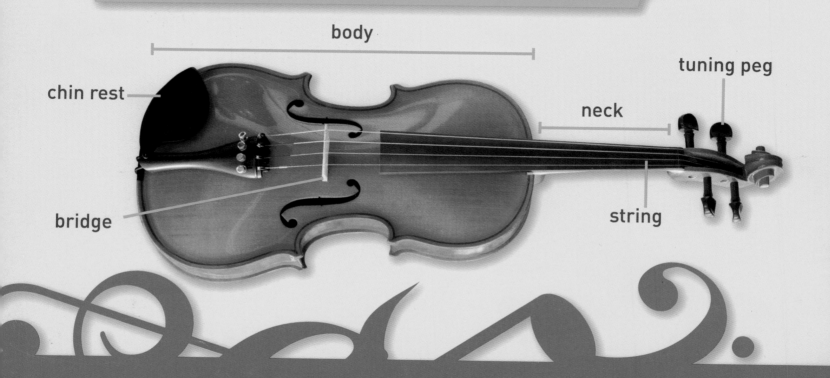

body

tuning peg

chin rest

neck

bridge

string

A violin bow is a long stick with a **strip** of horsehair **attached** to it. The hair is attached at the ends of the bow. The ends are called the head and the frog.

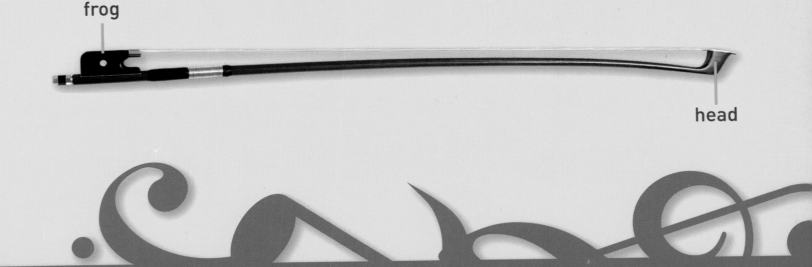

frog

head

The body of a full-size violin is about 14 inches (35 cm) long. Children **usually** learn on smaller violins.

There are also **electric** violins. Electric violins can have different shapes.

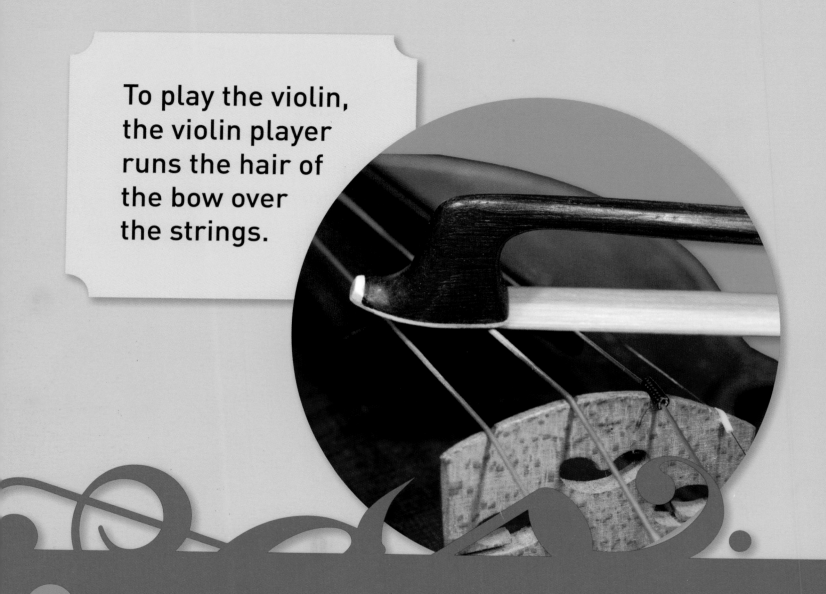

To play the violin,
the violin player
runs the hair of
the bow over
the strings.

The violin player presses the strings on the neck to play different notes.

Sometimes violin players **pluck** the strings with their fingers.

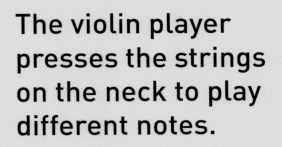

Let's Play

14

the Violin!

Wyatt's violin teacher is Ms. Evans. She shows Wyatt how to read notes on **sheet music**.

Alexa is at her violin **lesson**. Her teacher shows her how to hold the violin.

Madison just learned a new song on the violin. She wants to play it for her grandparents.

John practices the violin.
He is going to play in the
school talent show.

Find the Violin

a.

b.

c.

d.

a. clarinet

b. flute

c. guitar

d. violin [correct]

Violin Quiz

1. A violin bow has a **strip** of paper **attached** to it. True or False?

2. Children **usually** learn to play on small violins. True or False?

3. Violin players sometimes **pluck** the violin strings with their fingers. True or False?

4. Ms. Evans is Wyatt's violin teacher. True or False?

5. Madison wants to play her new song for her sister. True or False?

ANSWERS: 1. false 2. true 3. true 4. true 5. false

Glossary

attached – joined or connected.

electric – needing to be plugged into an outlet in order to work.

lesson – a period of time when a skill or topic is studied or taught.

main – the most important or the biggest.

pluck – to pull an instrument's strings with one's fingers.

sheet music – a sheet of paper with the notes to a song printed on it.

strip – a long, thin piece of something.

usually – commonly or normally.

DATE DUE

RADIOACTIVITY

HISTORY OF SCIENCE

RADIOACTIVITY

FROM THE CURIES
TO THE ATOMIC AGE

BY TOM McGOWEN

A GROLIER COMPANY

FRANKLIN WATTS
NEW YORK · LONDON · TORONTO
SYDNEY · 1986

Diagrams by Vantage Art

Photographs courtesy of:
AIP Niels Bohr Library/
W.F. Meggers Collection: p. 3;
AIP Niels Bohr Library:
pp. 7, 15, 24, 33, 44, 47, 53;
AIP Niels Bohr Library/
William G. Myers Collection: pp. 8, 11;
The Granger Collection: pp. 19, 41;
AIP Niels Bohr Library/
Donated by H. Richard Crane: p. 36;
Energy Research and Development
Administration: p. 51 (top left);
GA Technologies: p. 51 (top right);
University of California/Lawrence
Berkeley Laboratory: p. 51 (bottom).

Library of Congress Cataloging
in Publication Data

McGowen, Tom.
Radioactivity: from the Curies to the atomic age.
(History of science)
Bibliography: p.
Includes index.
Summary: Discusses discoveries, developments, and
scientists in the field of radioactivity, which
has revolutionized physics and medicine, with
particular emphasis on the work done by the Curies.
1. Radioactivity—History—Juvenile literature.
2. Curie, Marie, 1867–1934—Juvenile literature.
3. Curie, Pierre, 1859–1906—Juvenile literature.
4. Chemists—Poland—Biography—Juvenile literature.
[1. Radioactivity—History. 2. Curie, Marie, 1867–1934.
3. Curie, Pierre, 1859–1906] I. Title. II. Series:
History of science (Franklin Watts, inc.)
QC795.27.M38 1986   539.7'5'09   85-24684
ISBN 0-531-10132-0

CONTENTS

TO LONGTIME FRIEND
DEE HAAS

RADIOACTIVITY

CHAPTER

■

A MYSTERIOUS
GLOW

One of the most important sciences in the world today is the science called *physics*. The word *physics* means "natural things," and physics is the science that searches for, and studies, the natural laws and forces that make things happen—such things as water freezing into ice, a rainbow forming after a shower, the shining of the sun, the pull of a magnet. People who work in this field of science are called physicists. From the studies and discoveries of physicists have come a great many of the useful and enjoyable things we have today, such as telephones and television, air conditioning and automobiles, and electric lights and electronic computers.

In our modern world, the work of physicists is usually done in large, well-equipped laboratories, and the field of physics abounds with the possibilities for exciting new discoveries. But about a hundred years ago, near the end of the nineteenth century, things were very different. Only a few colleges and universities had real physics laboratories, and most physicists did their experimenting and studying in their homes. As for new discoveries, a great many physicists were convinced that all the exciting discoveries had already been made, and that all the natural laws and main principles of the universe had been explained. Physicists knew that heat, light, and sound were all

1 —

forms of energy, and that electricity and magnetism were related. From this knowledge had come such inventions as the steam engine, the telephone and telegraph, the electric motor, and the phonograph. Although most homes, places of work, and city streets were still lighted by gas lamps, the first power plant had been built and was generating electricity for a small part of New York City, and everyone knew the day would come when electric lighting would be everywhere. It didn't seem as if much was left to do.

Physicists knew of atoms, the tiny particles of which everything from air to water to rock to flesh is formed, but they thought of the atom as a kind of tiny, indestructible lump that was completely inactive and unchanging. The idea that there could be explosive energy in an atom would have made most physicists of a hundred years ago chuckle. No one even dreamed of such a possibility.

But in the last five years of the nineteenth century and the first few of the twentieth, a number of discoveries were made that suddenly changed scientists' minds about atoms and some other things. They were literally the first steps toward a new kind of world—the world in which *we* now live.

A RAY LABELED X

The first of these discoveries took place on a November afternoon in 1895, in the city of Würzburg, Germany. Wilhelm Roentgen, a fifty-year-old professor of physics at the University of Würzburg, was experimenting with a device known as a Crookes tube, when something astonishing happened.

The Crookes tube (named after William Crookes, the English physicist who invented it) was a pear-shaped glass bulb with most of the air pumped out of it and a pair of wires for carrying electricity stuck into it. The wire at one end was known as the cathode, or negative pole; the other, at the bottom, was the anode, or positive pole. When these wires were connected to a

2—

In Germany, Wilhelm Roentgen's research on cathode rays led to his discovery of X-rays in late 1895.

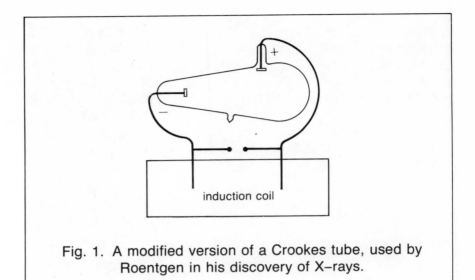

Fig. 1. A modified version of a Crookes tube, used by
Roentgen in his discovery of X–rays.

source of electric current, such as a generator, a patch of light
appeared inside the bulb, on the glass across from the cathode.
No one knew exactly why this happened.

For the experiment he was doing, Roentgen wanted to keep
this glow from showing, so he had made a box out of black cardboard and he put this over the Crookes tube. To make sure this
would completely cover up the glow, he pulled the drapes over
every window to darken the room, and peered down at the box
to see if any light was leaking through a crack or hole in it.

The box worked fine; no glow showed through it. But to
Roentgen's surprise he saw a glow of light coming from another
part of the room. Puzzled, he opened some of the drapes and
looked around to see what was causing the unexpected glow.

Several feet away from the box-covered Crookes tube, but
directly in line with it, was a sheet of paper fastened to a
wooden frame which Roentgen had prepared for another experi-

ment. The paper was coated with a mixture of chemicals that was phosphorescent—that is, the mixture would glow in the dark after it was exposed for a while to a bright light such as sunlight (the hands and numbers of watches and alarm clocks are often coated with phosphorescent chemicals so they can be seen in darkness). Roentgen quickly found that when he sent electricity into the Crookes tube with his hand-cranked generator, the chemical-coated paper would glow as if it had been put in a bright light. Obviously, *something*—some kind of beam or ray—was coming out of the Crookes tube, passing through the cardboard box, moving across several feet of air, and causing the chemical mixture on the paper to glow with phosphorescence!

Roentgen had no idea what the rays coming from the Crookes tube might be. In science, an unknown thing is often called by the letter *X*, so Roentgen began thinking of the rays as X-rays. He spent the next few days locked in his laboratory, experimenting to find out what X-rays could do. He put different materials and objects between the Crookes tube and the chemical-coated paper. If the paper glowed, Roentgen knew the rays had passed through whatever material was in front of the tube; if the paper didn't glow, he knew the rays had been stopped by the material. In this way he found out that the rays went through such things as wood, cloth, thin aluminum, and flesh, but were stopped by such things as thick lead and bone.

It occurred to Roentgen that since the mysterious rays acted like sunlight on the phosphorescent chemicals, they might also act like sunlight on photographic chemicals. In those days, photographic "film" was actually a square of thin glass that was coated on one side with chemicals that were sensitive to light, just as film is now. A coated glass of this sort was called a photographic plate. In the darkened room, Roentgen put an unexposed photographic plate in front of the Crookes tube and sent a flow of electric current into the tube. When he developed the photographic plate he saw that it was fogged, just as if it had been exposed to bright sunlight. He suddenly realized that X-rays could be used to take a certain kind of picture. He had his wife hold her hand between the Crookes tube and an unexposed photographic plate while he sent electricity into the tube. When he developed this plate he found himself looking at a shadowy picture of the bones that were inside her hand—the world's first X-ray picture. The X-rays had gone through his wife's flesh but had been stopped by the bones, and so the bones had cast a shadow on the photographic plate.

Roentgen knew he had discovered something important, but he didn't realize *how* important it was, for it was going to put the whole science of physics on a new path that would lead to discoveries and inventions no one had even dreamed of. And it was going to revolutionize the work of doctors. When Roentgen announced his discovery, doctors everywhere were quick to see what a tremendous help X-rays could be for them, and it wasn't long before many were using "Roentgen rays," as X-rays were called for a time, to literally look into their patients' bodies.

BECQUEREL'S GREAT DISCOVERY

Most nonscientific people were a bit fearful of these mysterious rays that could "look" inside human skin, but for physicists, X-rays presented an exciting new challenge that many of them began to think about and study. And this led to another accidental discovery that was tremendously important.

The man who made this discovery was a forty-four-year-old French physicist by the name of Antoine Henri Becquerel, a professor of physics at the Museum of Natural History in Paris. Becquerel was a member of a family that had already made many contributions to science. His grandfather had made important studies of magnetism and telegraphy and had been given an award for his work in electrochemistry. Becquerel's

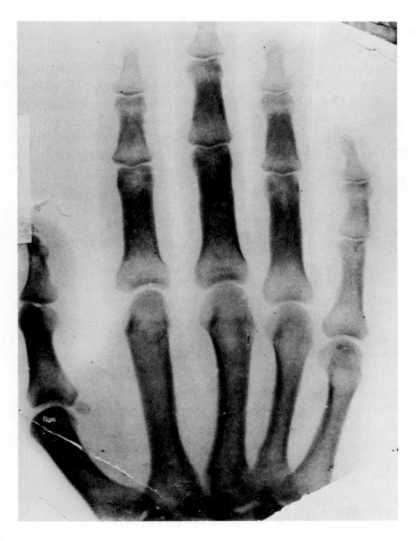

This is probably the first X-ray photograph taken in the United States. It was taken by F. R. Wolcott at the University of Wisconsin, and is of Wolcott's own hand.

BECQUERI

father had contributed to the knowledge of phosphorescence and photochemistry (the action of light on certain chemicals).

Becquerel was interested in trying to find out what caused phosphorescence, and when he read the reports of Roentgen's work with X-rays he began to wonder if phosphorescence might be a kind of X-ray. Roentgen had found that X-rays would fog a photographic plate, and Becquerel decided to see if phosphorescence would do the same.

He wrapped an unexposed photographic plate in black paper to protect it from light, and put it on a windowsill in bright sunlight. On top of it he placed a small amount of the phosphorescent material, called potassium uranyl sulfate, a chemical compound composed of sulfur and the metals potassium and uranium. The sunlight would cause this compound to become phosphorescent, and if phosphorescence *was* like X-rays, it would pass through the black paper and fog the photographic plate as a beam of light would do.

After a time, Becquerel unwrapped the plate and developed it. Sure enough, there was a dark splotch on it just where the phosphorescent chemical compound had been sitting. It certainly looked as if phosphorescence and X-rays had something in common.

Becquerel tried several more things just to make sure. He put a coin between the phosphorescent chemical and the black paper wrapped around a plate, and when he developed the plate, there was a dark circle just the size of the coin. This showed

A few months after Roentgen's discovery of X-rays, Antoine Becquerel, investigating the properties of X-rays and phosphorescence, discovered radioactivity.

that the rays given off by the phosphorescent material, like X-rays, wouldn't pass through fairly thick metal.

Then, to make sure that it *was* the phosphorescence at work, and not, perhaps, some sort of gas that was being created by the heat of the sun acting on the chemical, Becquerel put a piece of plain glass between the chemical and the paper-wrapped plate. Once again, the photographic plate had a black smudge on it when it was developed. A gas could not have gone through the piece of glass, so Becquerel now felt sure it was phosphorescence that was fogging the photographic plates. In a report of his experiments that he wrote for a French science magazine, he announced this discovery.

But Becquerel was going to find that he had made up his mind a little too quickly. A few days after making his experiments with the phosphorescent chemicals and photographic plates, he set out to make some new experiments with the same things, but along slightly different lines. He wrapped several photographic plates in black paper, but when he went to put them on the windowsill he found that it was a dark, rainy day without enough sunlight to affect the phosphorescent chemical compound. So he put the wrapped plates away in a drawer, with some of the chemical compound sitting on each of them, until the sun might come out again. However, the next three days were all dark and rainy too, so Becquerel finally just gave up in disgust, took the plates out of the drawer, and developed them. He didn't expect to find anything, so he was astounded to see that the plates were all fogged with dark splotches where the chemical compound had been sitting.

This should not have happened! The wrapped plates and chemicals had been inside a dark drawer for three days. The chemicals hadn't been touched by a bit of bright light and thus couldn't possibly have become phosphorescent enough to cause such dark marks on the plates. What had happened?

Becquerel thought it over. Had the chemicals managed to work in darkness, or had some light somehow gotten into the

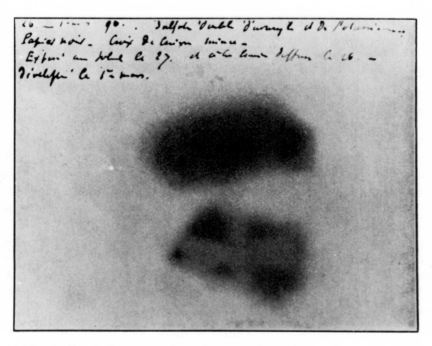

The fogged photographic plate, with Becquerel's notations, which led to his discovery of radioactivity

drawer? He had to find out for sure if the chemicals *could* work in the dark.

In a darkened room he put three uncovered, unexposed photographic plates into cardboard boxes. He covered one plate with a sheet of clear glass, one with a piece of thin aluminum, and left one uncovered. On the glass, the aluminum, and the uncovered plate he placed a bit of the phosphorescent chemical compound. Then he closed each box, put each box into another box, closed those, and put them all into a drawer. There was no way light could get to the chemicals through two boxes and the drawer.

After five hours, Becquerel developed the plates. Each showed a dark fog-mark where the chemical had been on it.

There was no way the chemicals could have become phosphorescent without light, so Becquerel now realized that it couldn't, after all, be phosphorescence that was fogging the plates. But then, what *was* doing it?

He thought about the chemical compound. It was what chemists called a "uranium salt," and there were several different kinds of uranium salts, all containing uranium combined with other things. Becquerel wondered if other uranium salts would also fog photographic plates as the one he had been using did.

He experimented with several different ones. They all fogged plates.

It was now obvious that what was happening must have something to do with the metal uranium itself. Becquerel got hold of some pure uranium and tried it on a photographic plate. The fog-mark it made was darker and sharper than any of the marks made by the uranium salt compounds.

So Becquerel was now able to report positively to his fellow physicists that the metal uranium gave off rays that could go through paper, glass, and thin aluminum, and that it did the same thing to a photographic plate that a glow of light would do. He had discovered what we now call *radioactivity*, which means "ray action," although he did not call it that, and didn't really understand what it was.

Neither did anyone else. Physicists all over the world were amazed by Becquerel's discovery. For radiation—the giving off of rays—to take place, there had to be an energy source. For example, a fire is the energy source for the heat that radiates away from it. But what was the energy source that enabled uranium to give off radiation? Naturally, it couldn't possibly be something in the lifeless metal itself; that idea was contrary to everything that nineteenth-century physicists believed to be true.

It was a problem that seemed to shout to be investigated, but surprisingly, not many scientists gave much attention to it. Most of them were still much more interested in X-rays, because you could make X-rays *do* things, whereas radioactivity didn't seem to have any use—it just happened.

However, a few physicists did become interested enough in radioactivity to begin looking into it. One of them was a twenty-nine-year-old Polish woman living in France. Her name was Marie Curie.

2

MARIA
SKLODOWSKA

The woman who was to become famous as Marie Curie was born Maria Sklodowska in Warsaw, Poland, in 1867. Unlike Roentgen, Becquerel, and most scientists who had easily been able to get into good universities and make their way into the field of science, this Polish girl had to struggle bitterly to achieve her goal of becoming a scientist. At the age of fifteen she graduated with top honors from high school, but while she desperately wanted to go on to college there was absolutely no way she could, for in the Russian Empire, of which Poland was then a part, women were simply not permitted to attend a university or to have any further education once they finished high school.

THE "FLOATING UNIVERSITY"

In order to continue her education, Maria took a dangerous chance. She began to go to what was called the "Floating University." These were classes in science and other subjects that were held secretly in the homes of teachers, in order to give young Poles such as Maria the kind of education they wanted, without Russian influence. But if the secret police learned of the classes, both the teachers and students would go to prison!

Maria Sklodowska arrived in Paris from Warsaw, Poland, at the age of twenty-four.

Maria attended the "Floating University" for more than a year, getting everything from it that she could. But this wasn't enough. She knew by then that what she wanted most of all was to become a physicist, but she simply couldn't learn enough science for that from the "Floating University." And even if she could, she could never work as a scientist in the Russian Empire—it wouldn't be allowed. So Maria came up with a desperate plan.

Her sister, Bronya, who was three years older, wanted to become a doctor as badly as Maria wanted to be a scientist, but that, too, would have been impossible in the Russian Empire. Bronya was saving money to go to France and study to be a doctor at a university there, but it was slow and dreadfully difficult to save enough. Now, however, seventeen-year-old Maria had her plan. She urged Bronya to take whatever money she had managed to save, and go at once to France. Meanwhile, Maria would get a job as a governess (a kind of full-time baby sitter and teacher for the young children of a wealthy family) and would send most of her pay to Bronya so that Bronya could live and study in France until she received her degree as a doctor. Then, once Bronya was a successful doctor, making money, she could send for Maria and pay her back by supporting her while she studied for *her* degree as a scientist.

Bronya finally saw that Maria's plan really offered the best chance for both of them. She left for Paris, and Maria, having just turned eighteen, went to work as a governess, living with a wealthy family in a small town far from Warsaw, teaching and caring for their small children.

JOURNEY TO PARIS

Four years passed. In Paris, Bronya had nearly completed her studies and would soon be a doctor. Meanwhile, she had married another Polish student she had met in medical school, who was just starting his career as a doctor. Bronya began sending letters to Maria, urging her to come live with them and enroll in the famous university known as the Sorbonne. But fearful that she might be a burden to Bronya and her husband, Maria held off for almost two more years, saving as much money as she could. Then, in 1891, at the age of twenty-four, she packed up all her belongings, bought the cheapest ticket possible on a railroad train that ran from Warsaw to Paris, and set out to make her dream of being a scientist come true at last. She arrived in Paris just in time to begin first-quarter courses at the Sorbonne.

The university was a new world for Maria. For the first time she had a chance to work in a real laboratory with first-class, up-to-date scientific instruments. She heard brilliant professors explain dazzling new ideas in physics and chemistry, ideas she had never even heard of in Poland. She realized how little she had been able to learn on her own. But she soaked up this new knowledge like a sponge, and tried to spend every minute of her spare time studying.

This wasn't always easy, because the home of Bronya and her husband, Casimir, where Maria was staying, was usually full of activity. Both Bronya and Casimir took care of their patients there, and Casimir was also fond of having parties. After a time, Maria decided she would be able to study better living by herself than living with her sister and brother-in-law, so she moved to a tiny room closer to the university.

The trouble with this was that with no one to look after her, Maria did almost nothing *but* study, often not even bothering to eat. Actually, there were many times when she simply couldn't afford to eat, for she barely had enough money to pay the monthly rent for her little room and to buy the books, paper, and other things she needed for school. So she was usually hungry. She was often cold, because she couldn't afford to buy enough coal to heat her little room. And she was generally overtired, because she would study until two or three o'clock in the morning, sleep only four or five hours, then hurry off to the university as early as possible.

But all this hard work and sacrifice paid off. In 1893, Maria —who was now using the French form of her name, Marie— took the test for a master's degree in physics and came in first in her class.

The school year was now over and Marie had gained her first goal, so she felt she could celebrate a bit. She scraped all her money together and went back for a summer-long visit to her home in Warsaw.

Marie enjoyed her vacation. But as time went on, she had to face the fact that she might not be able to go back to the Sorbonne to get the degree in mathematics she felt she needed. She simply did not have enough money left, and her father, who was living on a small pension, could not help her. As the beginning of the new school year grew nearer, Marie sadly began to give up her dream.

Then a miracle occurred. One of Marie's few friends, another Polish girl who had been studying at the Sorbonne, had gone to officials in Warsaw and told them about Marie Sklodowska, the girl who was at the top of her class but couldn't continue her schooling because of lack of money. The result was that Marie was given a scholarship, an award of six hundred rubles to enable her to go on with her studies at the Sorbonne! Thus, when the school year began in Paris, Marie was there.

A FATEFUL MEETING

Marie Sklodowska was now becoming noticed as a brilliant student and promising scientist, and early in 1894 she received her first scientific job—an organization called the Society for the Encouragement of National Industry hired her to see what she could find out about the magnetism of different kinds of steel. This was a marvelous piece of luck for Marie, but it gave

Pierre Curie lecturing at the Sorbonne.
When he met Maria Sklodowska he was already
a leading scientist in France.

her a problem, for she had no place where she could set up the equipment and make the tests that were needed—the room in which she lived was much too small. However, an acquaintance of hers, a Polish professor of physics who happened to be visiting Paris, came to her rescue. He introduced her to a young French scientist who was in charge of a large laboratory in which Marie could do her work. This French scientist was Pierre Curie, the man who was to become Marie's husband and her partner in great scientific discoveries.

Pierre Curie was a thirty-five-year-old professor at the School of Physics and Chemistry in Paris and a leading French scientist. He and his brother, who was also a physicist, were the discoverers of piezoelectricity, which is the production of an electric charge by a crystal (this played a part in the development of radio). Pierre also invented a scientific scale for very delicate work, and discovered an important fact of magnetism that is known to this day as Curie's Law.

Marie and Pierre were immediately attracted to each other. Within a year, they were married and settled in a small three-room apartment in Paris. And in 1897 Marie became a mother, giving birth to a baby daughter that was named Irene. Yet, even with all her work as a wife and mother, Marie still kept up with her studies of science. Each morning, while a hired nurse cared for little Irene, Marie worked in a laboratory at the School of Physics and Chemistry, doing research on problems that interested her.

Marie needed a special problem to work on, something she could investigate and write a report about, for in this way she could get her degree as a Doctor of Physics from the university. One of the things that interested her most was Antoine Henri Becquerel's discovery that uranium gave off radiation. Like most other physicists, both Marie and Pierre wondered where the energy for this radiation could be coming from. Marie decided to try to find out. She chose an investigation of uranium's radiation as the subject for her doctor's degree.

CHAPTER

IN A COLD,
DAMP
LABORATORY

The first step was to find a place where Marie could set up equipment and work in private. There was no room in the Curie's little apartment, and they couldn't afford to rent a special room anywhere, nor could Marie use the laboratory at the School of Physics and Chemistry, for too many other people were always using it for many different things. But on the ground floor of the school building there was a small storeroom that wasn't being used, and Pierre managed to get permission from the director of the school for Marie to use that. It was tiny and cramped, damp and unheated, and it had no electric outlets, but it was the best Marie could get, and she was glad to have it.

The second step was to get the instruments and equipment Marie would need for her tests and experiments. She solved that problem with her own brilliant mind. Pierre owned an electrometer, an instrument for measuring electric charges, and Marie figured out how to use it to test for radiation. She knew that Becquerel, in his experiments with uranium, had found that radiation was accompanied by an electric charge, so she used the electrometer to measure the electric charge that was coming from all the compounds of uranium she tested, and this gave her a way of also measuring the strength of the radiation. The other instruments she used—a scale, a thermometer, and so on—were also things she and Pierre owned; thus, she simply made do with what she had. From scientist friends she was able to borrow the uranium compounds and other chemicals that she needed for her tests.

So she set to work. But working in the little storeroom turned out to be far from easy. Checking the temperature in the place one cold winter day, she found it was six degrees below freezing! Such cold, and dampness, often affected the instruments Marie was using, so that they wouldn't work quite right, and she would have to make allowances for that. She herself was often uncomfortably cold, and afflicted with sniffles. Despite all this she steadfastly kept working, and within a few weeks she had managed to find out several important facts.

One was that the radiation given off by uranium was steady and even. It didn't stop and start, it didn't change from strong to weak; it was always the same. Marie also found that the radiation wasn't affected by anything that might be done to the uranium. Whether the uranium was made cold as ice or burning hot, whether it was wet or dry, if it was kept under steady, bright light or in total darkness, the radiation stayed the same.

This told Marie that whatever was causing the radiation was in the uranium itself; it wasn't coming from "stored-up" sunlight or heat, as some scientists had suggested. Marie began to wonder if perhaps the radiation didn't have something to do with the very atoms that formed the element uranium.

This was a rather startling idea. Like other scientists of that time, Marie knew that all matter—all gases, liquids, and solids, on earth and everywhere else in the universe—were formed of particles called atoms, so tiny that it took billions of them to make something the size of a speck of dust. It was also known then that there are many different kinds of atoms, and each kind forms a substance that science calls an element; thus, a certain kind of atom forms the shiny, yellow metal element we call gold, another kind forms the colorless, odorless, tasteless gas element we call oxygen, and so on. But while nineteenth-century scientists recognized that there were different kinds of atoms, they believed that all atoms were alike in that they were merely inert "building blocks." Marie, however, was beginning to wonder if there might not be something different about a uranium atom that made uranium the only element that gave off radiation.

But then she was struck by the thought that maybe uranium was *not* the only element that gave off radiation. Maybe others did. Maybe they all did! As far as she knew, no one had ever checked to find this out. At once, she decided she must do so.

So she went to work on the tremendous task of testing every known chemical substance for radiation; from chunks of pure elements such as lead and copper, to complicated compounds made up of several different elements. She found one other element that gave off radiation—the soft, silvery metal called thorium, which, in the 1800s, was used in the manufacture of gas lamps.

It was Marie Curie who now invented the word *radioactivity* for the radiation given off by uranium and thorium. In the notes she was keeping about her experiments she called uranium and thorium "radio elements." She began working only with compounds that contained one of these elements, testing to see how much radiation they gave off.

This led to a sensational discovery. Marie found that two of the compounds she was testing—an ore called pitchblende, which contained uranium, and an ore called chalcolite, which contained thorium—seemed to give off a lot more radiation than could be accounted for by the amounts of uranium and thorium that were in them. Thinking she had made a mistake, Marie did her tests over. She got the same result. She did the tests over again, ten times. Same result. She talked to a few other scientists who told her she must have made an error, and

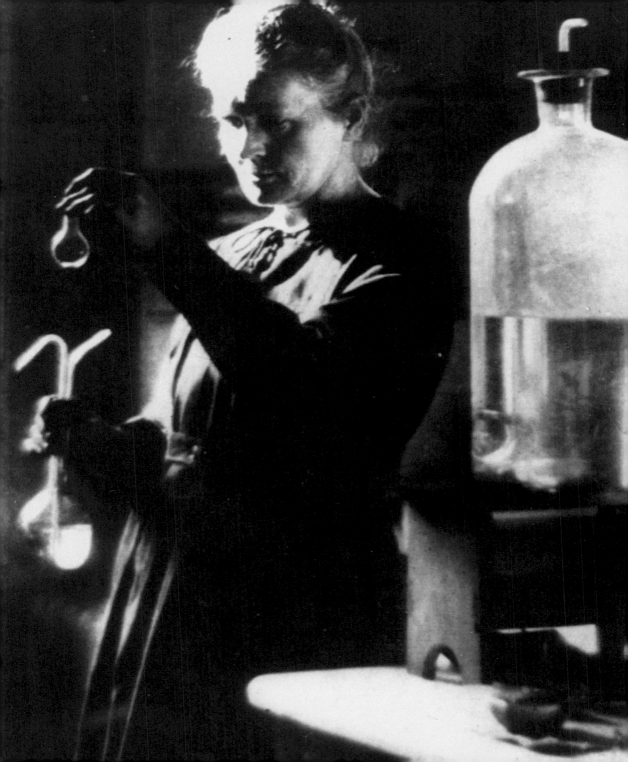

should check her tests again. She did—ten more times. The results were always the same. She was definitely getting more radiation than she should have been getting.

There was only one possible explanation. There had to be something else besides uranium or thorium in each of these compounds, something that was giving off powerful radiation of its own. But Marie had already checked every known element for radiation. If there was something other than uranium or thorium here, giving off radiation, it could only be a new, unknown radioactive element!

Although Pierre Curie had not been helping Marie with her project, he had been carefully following her work, talking with her about it and reading all her notes. It now looked to him as if she were on the verge of a major scientific discovery. Pierre had been working on a project of his own, in which he was tremendously interested, but he felt that what Marie was doing was so important that he dropped his own work in order to help her. So, two brilliant minds were now focused on the problem of tracking down the new element.

POLONIUM IS DISCOVERED

It was on April 14, 1898, that Pierre and Marie began working together. That morning, working with an approximate 3.5 ounce (100 grams) chunk of pitchblende, they began taking turns

Marie Curie in her laboratory.
Equipped with only a few simple
instruments, but with brilliant
reasoning powers, she began the
search for the source of uranium's
radiation, which resulted in the
discovery of a new element, polonium.

grinding it into powder. Pitchblende is a black or dark brown, rocklike substance with a dull shine like tar, and is a compound of uranium, oxygen, and a number of other elements in tiny amounts. What the Curies intended to do was separate all the elements from one another until they had the one that was unknown, all by itself. They dissolved the ground-up pitchblende in acid, and Marie began the long, slow job of separating the elements, using the methods known to chemists in those days.

It wasn't until almost two months later that the husband and wife saw they were closing in on their goal. On June 6, Marie put a small amount of a chemical into a beaker of liquid and watched as a powdery solid material began to separate from the liquid and sink to the bottom of the beaker. After enough of this muddy stuff had collected, Marie spooned some of it out and tested it for radiation. It was 150 times more radioactive than an equal amount of uranium!

The substance definitely contained the new element, but the element was mixed with a large amount of another element called bismuth, and the Curies had to get rid of that. Pierre put a small amount of the substance into a test tube which he then heated over the flame of a bunsen burner—a metal pipe connected to a gas outlet. As the test tube got hotter and hotter the thick, muddy liquid began to bubble, and a black, sooty powder started forming on the glass sides of the tube above the liquid. Pierre kept heating the tube until it cracked, then he scraped off some of the black powder and tested it. The radioactivity for such a tiny bit of material was extremely high. Pierre had managed to "cook off" much of the bismuth, and the Curies were getting closer to producing a pure amount of the new element.

By the end of June they decided they were close enough. There was still a lot of bismuth in the substance they now had, but the substance tested 330 times more radioactive than an equal amount of uranium. There was no doubt but that it contained a major amount of the new element.

"You will have to name it," Pierre told his wife. Although he had helped her find this new element, it was really her discovery, so it was hers to name.

"Could we call it 'polonium'?" she suggested after a moment. She named the new element after her native land, Poland.

THE SEARCH FOR RADIUM

So, with her husband's help, Marie Curie had discovered a new element. But the Curies' work was far from over. While they had been working to separate the polonium from the other elements in the pitchblende they had noticed that the portion of pitchblende containing an element called barium also had a high amount of radiation—again, much higher than could be accounted for by the amount of uranium present. Both Marie and Pierre believed this could only mean that polonium was not the *only* new radioactive element hidden away in pitchblende. There was another new element, and just as polonium was closely linked with bismuth, this other element seemed to be linked with barium.

The Curies quickly prepared a report of their discovery of polonium and sent it to the French Academy of Science. Then they took a short vacation in the country, taking baby Irene with them. Chances are, as they strolled through the woods and rode their bicycles along country roads, they talked of the other new element they thought they had found.

When the Curies returned to Paris they began working with the portion of the pitchblende material containing barium, which they had put aside while they worked to separate out the polonium. Now, they repeated the work they had done with the bismuth and polonium. They slowly managed to separate the barium from the rest of the compound, and after weeks of work they had a substance that was mostly barium, but which they felt sure contained the second new element as well. When they tested it, they found it was 900 times more radioactive than a similar amount of uranium. The new element was definitely present!

In December, together with a physicist named Gustave Bemont, who helped them separate out the barium compound, the Curies wrote another report for the Academy of Science. The three scientists announced their belief that they had found another new radioactive element, which they had decided to call *radium.* They reported that it was many, many more times radioactive than uranium.

But now a problem came up. A good many scientists, especially chemists, wanted to *see* an actual sample of pure radium. They wanted to figure out the atomic weight of radium, so they could fit it into the official list known as the periodic table of elements. Until they could do this, many of them were not willing to accept that radium actually existed.

So Marie and Pierre were faced with the need to produce at least a few grams of pure or nearly-pure radium for chemists to weigh and examine. But the Curies had found that the amounts of radium and polonium in pitchblende were incredibly tiny. They knew that in order to get even a few ounces of radium they would have to start with tons of pitchblende. And this presented a serious problem, because the Curies simply did not have enough money to buy a large amount of the ore, which was rather expensive. Nor could they get any help from the government, for in those days governments did not give money to scientists as they do now, even though the scientists were doing important work.

Were the Curies and their discoveries to be ignored, simply because of poverty?

THE YEARS OF
HARD WORK

In the nineteenth century, a scientist working on a project was like an artist working on a painting or a writer working on a book. To such people, their work was the most important thing in their lives, and they wouldn't let anything, not even poverty, illness, or hunger, keep them from finishing it. So the Curies did not even consider giving up. It did not matter in the least to them that they were really too poor to be able to afford the material they needed to finish their work; the only problem they would consider was how to get what they needed with the small amount of money they had.

Pierre Curie began writing letters to chemists, laboratories, and factories that produced chemicals, trying to find someone who could supply him and Marie with at least a ton of pitchblende as cheaply as possible. But no one had nearly enough of the ore to send the Curies what they needed.

PITCHBLENDE FROM AUSTRIA

One day the Curies learned of a mine in Austria, where tons of pitchblende were dug out of the earth, the uranium was removed (it was used in the manufacture of colored glass at that time), and the remainder then simply thrown away. This seemed perfect for the Curies' needs; not only would they be saved a lot of time by not having to remove the uranium from the ore themselves, but with the uranium gone from it the ore was practically valueless and the Curies would probably be able to buy it at a very low price. They got in touch with an Austrian scientist they knew and asked him to help them find out what the Austrian government, which owned the mine, would charge them for a ton of the cast-off pitchblende, and what the cost would be to have it shipped to Paris.

But the Austrian did better than that. Knowing the importance of the work the Curies were doing, he talked the Austrian government officials into letting them have the pitchblende for nothing. They would have to pay only for the shipping. Even this would take a big bite out of the Curies' tiny savings, but it was far less than they had thought they would have to spend, and they were delighted.

THE EXPERIMENT BEGINS

But now that the pitchblende problem was solved, the Curies again had to deal with the problem of a place to do their work, for the little storeroom they had been using as a laboratory was much too small for a project involving a ton of ore. They tried to get a room in the Sorbonne, but nothing was available. They thought of renting a shed somewhere, but couldn't find anything they could afford.

Again, the director of the School of Physics and Chemistry came to their aid. On the school grounds was an old shed which he told the Curies they could use. It was actually in even worse shape than the little storeroom—there was a hole in the roof, which leaked when it rained—but it was large enough and it contained several rickety old tables and an old cast-iron stove. The Curies gladly accepted it.

A few weeks later, a big, horse-drawn wagon, bearing a load of bulging sacks, rumbled to a stop on the street outside the

School of Physics and Chemistry. The pitchblende had arrived from Austria. Pierre and Marie were notified and came hurrying out to oversee the unloading and storing of the sacks in their shed. Marie couldn't keep from opening one of the bags and plunging her hand into the ore. Locked away in this gritty, dark-brown stuff that was mixed with pine needles from the ground on which it had been dumped, was her new element, radium.

Once again the husband and wife went to work, with Marie doing the chemistry of separating the elements and Pierre doing the physics of studying and recording each chemical compound that was produced. But this time the work was much harder in every way, and for Marie it was actual *toil*. For hours at a time she had to stir big pots of boiling liquid, then the liquid had to be poured into large jars and lugged into the shed. Most of the boiling had to be done outside the shed, in the school court-yard, for otherwise the shed became filled with bad-smelling smoke that made breathing difficult. When it rained, Marie and Pierre had to drag the pots inside and leave the doors and windows wide open, working in the smelly smoke as best they could.

Actually, working outside the shed wasn't really much worse than working inside it. Even when the little stove was so loaded with coal that it glowed red hot, it didn't give off enough heat to warm the shed, and on a winter day the shed was nearly as cold inside as outside. In the summertime the shed seemed to gather in heat like a sponge, and became stifling. Winter or summer, when there was rain the roof leaked, and the two scientists had to be careful where they put their instruments and containers of chemicals, so that rain wouldn't fall on them.

THE "HAPPIEST YEARS"

It seems incredible now, when most scientists work in clean, heated, and air-conditioned laboratories, that two such great scientists as Marie and Pierre Curie should have had to do such important work under such dreadful conditions. Even a scientist of their own time, a famous German chemist who, much later, came to see their "laboratory," was astounded that they could have done such great things in such a place.

The work was not only difficult, it also took a long time. The Curies did have some help. From time to time, apparently as often as he could, a man who worked as an assistant in the school laboratory came to work with the Curies after hours. His name was Petit, and he worked without pay, simply for the chance to be a part of what he may have felt would be a great scientific achievement. But the greatest part of the work was still done by Marie. Her days of boiling, stirring, and pouring dragged into weeks, then months, as she gradually separated compounds containing radium and polonium from the rest of the elements in the pitchblende. The first ton of the ore turned out to be far from enough, so the Curies had to get more, and that, too, had to be boiled and stirred and poured off and separated out. Months turned into *years* of continuous, grinding work— four years altogether, from the time the Curies first began, to the moment when they finally had a small but measurable amount of nearly pure radium.

Yet despite all this truly backbreaking work and the dreadful discomforts of the shed, those four years were apparently the most joyful time of Marie Curie's life, and probably of Pierre's, too. Twenty years later, Marie wrote, "it was in this miserable old shed that the best and happiest years of our life were spent, entirely consecrated to work." She and Pierre were happy because they were doing something they were intensely interested in and knew was tremendously important. They felt at home working in the shed. As they would wait for a kettle of liquid to boil, or for a chemical change to take place, they would walk back and forth, talking about their work and what it might mean to the future. When the cold of winter seeped into the shed they would huddle by the small and all-but-useless stove, and share a cup of tea in cozy comradeship.

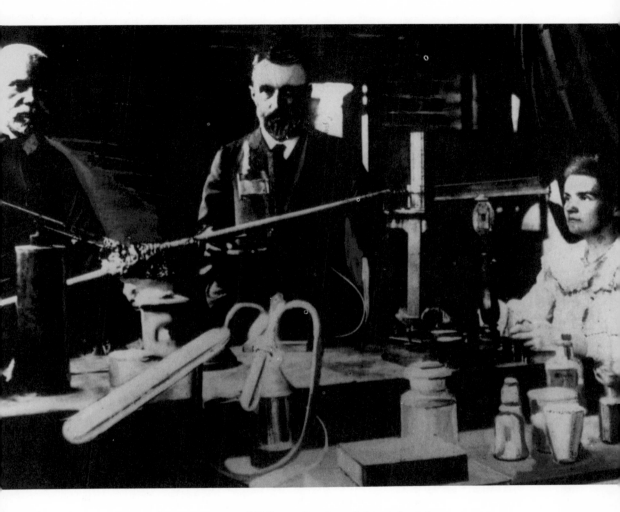

*The Curies and Edison Petit, a lab technician,
making a measurement of radioactivity.*

But about halfway through their four years of work, the Curies almost gave up both the shed and the work. They had gained a high reputation throughout Europe, and in July of 1900 the head of the University of Geneva, Switzerland, came to Paris to try to talk them into becoming teachers at his university. He offered them a salary that was a great deal more than the money they were managing to make in Paris, and even offered to have a special laboratory built for them, exactly as they wanted it. This was very tempting, of course, and Pierre, at least, was ready to accept.

However, when the heads of the Sorbonne, the university in Paris, learned that the Curies might leave France they quickly made an offer of their own to the two scientists—an important job for Pierre and a part-time job for Marie, which would bring them a lot more money. It really wasn't quite as good an offer as the Swiss one, but the Curies decided to accept it. Their main reason for accepting was that they simply didn't want to stop doing the work in the shabby shed, which was so important to them. So they stayed in France and went on with their beloved task of finding out as much as they could about radium and radioactivity.

A DEADLY ENEMY

Although the Curies weren't aware of it, this work that they loved so much was actually harmful to them. No one then knew there was such a thing as radiation sickness, but the Curies' years of work with radioactive materials had given them this dreadful disease. Their bodies had soaked up a steady bombardment of radiation and they began to suffer for it. They seemed to always be tired—much more tired than they should have been even from the hard work they were doing. More and more often, either Pierre or Marie would feel unwell and would be unable to work. Radiation had damaged their blood and bones and body organs. Luckily for their happiness and peace of mind they didn't know this, and didn't know that the very thing they most enjoyed doing was slowly poisoning them. (Pierre Curie was killed in an accident in 1906, but Marie eventually died of leukemia, cancer of the blood, which was almost certainly caused by her years of exposure to radiation.)

As time went on and they were getting closer to finally producing a bit of nearly-pure radium, Marie grew more and more excited. "I wonder what it will be like, what it will look like?" she said to her husband one evening. "Pierre, what form do you imagine it will take?"

"I don't know," he replied. He thought about it for a moment or two. He and Marie knew that radium was a metal, of course, but would it have the dull blackness of iron, the orange gleam of copper, the frosted luster of silver? "I should like it to have a beautiful color," he said seriously.

As days went by, the containers and test tubes on the old tables in the shed were filling with compounds that were closer and closer to pure radium. But this was a difficult time, for as Marie grew closer to producing pure radium her containers were in greater danger of being polluted. Soot, ashes, coal dust, and other things drifted into the shed through the broken roof, and became mixed with the materials in the test tubes the instant they were uncovered. Worse still, the slightest accidental bump to one of the rickety tables might knock a container onto the floor to smash and spill its precious contents. This happened several times! Marie Curie must have longed for a spotlessly clean laboratory and well-protected equipment with which to finish her work, but she grimly continued with what she had.

On March 28, 1902, Marie believed she had finally reached her goal. She had a tiny amount of material that she felt sure was nearly all radium with little or no barium left in it. She took this sample to a man name Eugene Demarcay, a scientist who was a good friend of the Curies, and who owned a spectroscope, an instrument that can measure the amount of every

element that is in any substance. (The atoms of every element give off light when the element is heated to high temperature, and the pattern of light is different for every element. A spectroscope spreads out the light from a heated substance, showing every pattern that is given off.) When Demarcay examined the sample he found mainly a strong, new pattern, a trace of barium pattern, and nothing else. Marie's substance was nearly-pure radium, positive proof that the new element really existed.

So the four years of hard work and discomfort were over. That night, after Marie put little Irene to bed, she went downstairs and found Pierre walking slowly about the room, his mind obviously on something. Marie sat down for a time—but could not stay put. Rising, she said, "Suppose we go down there for a moment?"

Pierre knew what she meant. She wanted to go to the shed, where their containers of radium were. So did he; that was what he had been thinking about. Quickly, they put on their coats and went out. They hurried down the dark, quiet streets to the Rue Lhomond, on which stood the School of Physics and Chemistry. They crossed the courtyard to the dark shed. Pierre took a key from his pocket, unlocked the shed door, and pushed it open. It squeaked, as it always did. Together, Marie and Pierre entered the shed.

"Look!" exclaimed Marie. "Look!"

In the darkness, the tiny quantities of the radioactive element, radium, in their glass containers, were glowing with a pale blue light.

This English caricature of the Curies depicts a dramatic moment in history as Marie and Pierre discover that radium gives off a pale blue light.

THE SOURCE
OF RADIATION
IS FOUND

Pure radium is a silvery-white metal, but radium is never found in its pure form; it has to be separated out of the uranium ore in which it is contained. Even then it is seldom truly pure, usually being combined in a compound called radium chloride, or radium salt, which looks much like ordinary table salt. It is extremely rare; in a ton of uranium ore there may be only one-two hundredth of an ounce (150 mgs) of radium. Naturally, it is very costly, and even today, one ounce (28 grams) of radium can cost more than a million dollars! But it is quite useful and valuable, for its radiation is helpful in treating certain kinds of cancer, tumors, and skin diseases, and is also used for a number of scientific purposes.

As a result of the work she had done in discovering the existence of radium and separating it out of tons of pitchblende, Marie Curie was given her degree as a Doctor of Physical Science by the University of Paris on June 25, 1903. In December of that same year, the Academy of Science in Stockholm, Sweden, announced that the Nobel Prize in Physics—the highest award there is for scientific work in physics—was being jointly awarded to Antoine Henri Becquerel and Pierre and Marie Curie. (Two years earlier, Wilhelm Roentgen had re-

ceived the first Nobel Prize for physics ever given, for his discovery of X-rays.)

The Curies now began to be showered with awards and
honors. Their discoveries of polonium and radium had aroused
the interest and excitement of physicists and chemists. One
scientist, warned by his doctor that he was ill and might die,
protested that he simply couldn't die yet, because he wanted
to know more about radium!

One of the things Pierre Curie had found out from his four-
year-long investigation of radium's radioactivity was that three-
hundredths of an ounce (one gram, or about as much as a paper
clip weighs) of radium pours out more than 100 calories of heat
an hour. That is enough heat to bring a gram of water to a boil.
Pierre also found, by strapping to his arm a packet containing a
tiny amount of radium salt, that the rays given off by radium
would burn human skin. And both he and Marie had seen that
radium gave off light, shining in the dark with a pale blue
radiance. Where was the energy that produced all this heat and
light coming from? This question still baffled every physicist in
the year the Curies finished their work with radium.

THEORIES PROVED
AND DISPROVED

Naturally, there were plenty of ideas. A famous English scientist suggested that radium and polonium got their energy by
somehow soaking up "ethereal waves" that were in the air—
although he could not, of course, prove that such waves existed,
nor even tell what they were. Marie Curie still had the idea that
the source of the energy was connected to the radium itself,
and she wrote a report suggesting that perhaps radiation was
actually tiny particles of radium that were being thrown off. She
was almost right.

The idea that rays might actually be tiny particles of some-

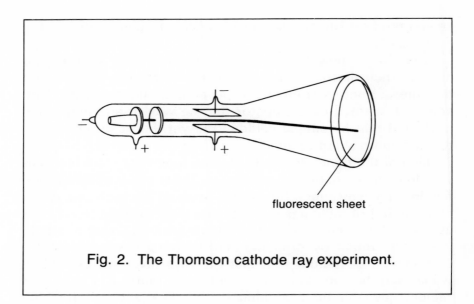

fluorescent sheet

Fig. 2. The Thomson cathode ray experiment.

thing had occurred to a number of scientists. In fact, back in 1879, Sir William Crookes, the inventor of the Crookes tube, had decided that the rays which caused the mysterious glow of light in his tubes were streams of molecules that had electric charges. (A molecule is a tiny particle made up of one or more atoms of something.) That theory had caused a lot of argument because a number of scientists felt sure that the rays, which were known as cathode rays, were actually caused by a mysterious unknown substance mixed with the air inside the tubes. In 1896, an English physicist named Joseph J. Thomson decided the rays must be streams of some kind of particle that came out of a tube's cathode, or negative electric pole. Thomson built a special cathode ray tube that had a metal wall with a thin slit in it right in front of the cathode, so that if particles *were* coming out of the cathode they would be forced to go through the

England's Joseph John Thomson demonstrated that a cathode ray was a stream of negatively charged particles, later known as electrons.

slit and would come out of it in a thin straight line. Farther up inside the tube were two pieces of electrically charged metal, directly across from each other. A stream of something going between these metal plates would thus be passing through an electric field, and if the stream was made up of particles that had a negative electric charge, as Thomson felt sure, the electric field would cause the stream to *bend*. To see if it bent, Thomson put a flat sheet coated with fluorescent chemicals at the end of the tube. Where the rays struck the chemical they would cause a glowing spot, and if that spot were on the upper part of the sheet, rather than in the middle, it would show that the rays were being bent.

Thomson generated electricity into his tube. A glowing spot appeared on the upper part of the fluorescent sheet.

So Thomson had proved that a cathode ray was a stream of negatively charged particles. He called these particles "corpuscles," but they were later named *electrons*, which is what they are still called today. By means of mathematics Thomson was able to figure out how big such particles must be, and because they were so incredibly tiny it seemed to him that they could only be *parts* of atoms. He decided that an atom must be a kind of blob of positive electrical energy packed full of a number of electrons—somewhat like a watermelon full of seeds. That was completely wrong, of course, but at least Thomson had shown that there was something smaller than an atom and that it was streams of these subatomic particles that formed the rays that came from a Crookes tube.

About a year later, Antoine Becquerel heard about Thomson's work and decided to try the same sort of experiment on the rays that were given off by uranium. He got exactly the same results as Thomson. This meant that uranium rays, too, must be streams of electrons.

So scientists were beginning to find out what radiation was. But what *caused* it was more of a mystery than ever. How could these "loose" electrons be coming out of uranium? What was making them come out? Why was it happening?

RUTHERFORD'S ALPHA AND BETA RAYS

At about the same time that Becquerel was performing his experiment, one of the scientists who was finally going to solve the puzzle was working toward the solution in a laboratory at McGill University in Canada. He was the physicist Ernest Rutherford.

Rutherford was born in New Zealand in 1871. He was one of twelve children, and his parents scrimped and saved and did without things for themselves in order to see that all their children were well educated. Their efforts paid off, because Ernest Rutherford, given the opportunity, turned out to be a brilliant student in high school and college, winning prizes and scholarships. He was also an outstanding athlete and a well-liked, popular person. He graduated from college with top honors in physics and mathematics, just as Marie Curie had. He worked for a while as a teacher, then won a scholarship that enabled him to continue his education at Cambridge University in England. There he studied physics, and one of his teachers was Professor Joseph J. Thomson. Rutherford worked with Thomson on a special experiment and did some important and useful work on his own.

Rutherford became interested in radioactivity at just about the same time the Curies did, and he began working with uranium, trying to find out exactly how powerful its radiation was. This led him to the discovery, in 1899, that uranium actually gave off two different kinds of radiation. One kind, which Rutherford named *Alpha rays*, after the first letter of the Greek alphabet, could be stopped by a very thin sheet of aluminum, but the other kind, which he called *Beta rays*, after the second

*New Zealand physicist Ernest Rutherford won
the Nobel Prize for chemistry in 1908 for
his pioneer work on the nature of the atom.*

Greek letter, would pass right through even very thick pieces of metal and other materials.

In 1899 Rutherford began working with the radioactive metal thorium and quickly found that it, too, gave off Alpha and Beta rays. Robert B. Owens, an American scientist who was working in the McGill laboratory at that time, noticed that the rays coming from thorium seemed to move about, almost as if they were being blown by wind, which was impossible. Trying to find out why this happened, Rutherford found that thorium gave off a radioactive *gas*, and it was the flowing movement of this gas that made it seem as if the radiation were being blown about. Rutherford also found that anything the gas touched would become radioactive. He collected quantities of the gas, which he called "thorium emanation," for study, and learned that its radioactivity grew weaker and weaker as time went on, until it was all but gone. Making careful measurements he found that the radioactivity of thorium emanation became fifty percent weaker (half as strong) every fifty-four seconds. Because the activity, or "life," of the radiation was steadily being cut in half, Rutherford used the term *half-life* to describe this slow weakening. While this was an interesting discovery, it didn't seem to be particularly important at the time. But it would be, later.

Rutherford wrote reports on his discoveries about thorium emanation, and they were published in scientific magazines in 1900. A short time later, a man named Frederick Soddy came to McGill University as a teacher in the chemistry department. Rutherford and Soddy, the two men who were going to solve the mystery of radioactivity, had now come together.

Frederick Soddy was born in England in 1877. As a young man he went to Oxford University and quickly found that he had a tremendous interest in chemistry. After graduating, he jumped at the chance to take a rather low-paying teaching job at McGill University because he had heard that McGill had an extremely well-equipped chemistry laboratory. Soddy became acquainted with Rutherford and grew interested in the work he was doing on radioactivity, soon joining in on it. He had a much greater knowledge of chemistry than Rutherford had, and was able to suggest many ways of using chemistry to help Rutherford do his work. It was a simple chemical process that put the two men on the track that led to the discovery of what radioactivity is.

Soddy had used the simple process to separate thorium from some other material that had been mixed in with it. Then he and Rutherford were astounded to find that the nearly-pure thorium Soddy had obtained was hardly giving off any radiation at all. Quickly, they checked the material that had been taken out of the thorium. *It* was extremely radioactive!

It seemed as if this material, which had been part of the thorium, was actually what was radioactive, and not the thorium at all. Soddy tested the substance and found that it was different, with different characteristics, from thorium. They named it "thorium X."

It was now time for the university to close down for the Christmas vacation, so Rutherford and Soddy put away their quantities of thorium and thorium X and left. When they returned, weeks later, they checked the substances to see if anything had happened to them. To their astonishment, they found that the thorium X was now hardly radioactive at all, while the thorium, which had not been very radioactive before, was now giving off powerful radiation.

CHANGING "LEAD INTO GOLD"

Why had this happened and what could it mean? The two men determined that thorium X had a half-life, just as thorium emanation did, and its radiation had slowly weakened. But then, why didn't that radiation weaken while thorium X was still part of thorium? The only answer was that it *did*—but that new quantities of it, with strong radiation, were *continuously being created*. This was why the thorium was now powerfully radioactive again; some of it had turned into new thorium X. This could only

Rutherford's research room at the Cavendish Laboratory, Cambridge, England, later in his career.

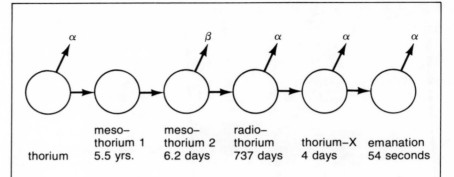

Fig. 3. Thorium transmutation. This diagram shows thorium's half–life, demonstrating that it is the loss of particles that causes atoms to change and that when an atom loses a number of its particles it becomes a different kind of atom.

mean that some of the thorium atoms had changed into atoms of thorium X!

This was an absolutely sensational discovery. Rutherford and Soddy had just proved wrong the nineteenth-century beliefs that atoms were inert, unchanging objects, and that no new matter had been formed since the creation of the earth. Frederick Soddy later said that he was "overwhelmed by something greater than joy," to realize that he had helped discover things no one had believed possible. In medieval times, men known as alchemists had tried to find a magic way of changing one kind of substance into another, especially lead into gold, and this had been called "transmutation." Modern nineteenth-century scientists paid no attention to such magical nonsense. But now . . . "Rutherford," Soddy exclaimed to his co-worker, "this is transmutation!"

"For Mike's sake, Soddy, don't call it transmutation," protested Rutherford. "They'll have our heads off as alchemists!" He apparently feared that other scientists would simply make fun of him and Soddy if the two of them claimed to have found what medieval magicians had been looking for.

But it *was* transmutation, for the thorium was changing into something else. Within a year, Rutherford had figured out exactly what was happening, and was able to announce to the scientists of the world what radiation is—the splitting off of tiny particles of atoms, which then go hurtling away at tremendous speed. It is the energy released by the activity of these particles as they explode free that produces the heat and light of radiation which had baffled the Curies and other scientists. Rutherford also figured out that it was the loss of particles which caused atoms to change, for when an atom loses a number of its particles it becomes a different kind of atom; an atom of a different *element*. Rutherford was able to show that when a uranium atom lost particles it became a radium atom; the radium atom lost particles and became a polonium atom; and the polonium atom lost particles and became an atom of lead, which then stayed the same, for the lead atom is "stable" (unchanging) and does not shoot off any particles. Thus, Rutherford also showed that the radioactive elements radium and polonium were different forms of the element uranium. (Thorium, too, changes into different forms.)

Rutherford was thirty-two years old when he published his explanation of radioactivity in 1903. A great many scientists, especially chemists, simply did not accept his explanation at first. They still believed that atoms were unchangeable, and, just as Rutherford had feared, they looked upon the idea of atoms coming apart and turning into new matter as medieval alchemy. But within a short time Rutherford piled up so much evidence that no one could have doubts any longer. In 1908 he was awarded a Nobel Prize. (Frederick Soddy also later won a Nobel Prize for research on radioactivity.)

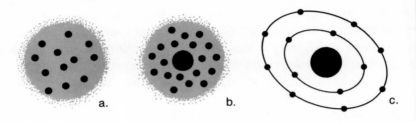

Fig. 4. (a) Thomson theorized that the atom was a mass of positive electrical energy packed full of a number of electrons. (b) Rutherford proposed that the atom consisted of a thick cluster of particles, the positively charged nucleus, with a number of other particles—electrons—orbiting it in arbitrary patterns. (c) Later, scientists came to believe that the particles that orbited the nucleus did so in a fixed pattern.

But it was in 1911 that Rutherford made his greatest contribution to science when he worked out the structure of an atom—a thick cluster of particles, the nucleus, with a number of other particles moving around it, somewhat like planets moving around a sun. We now know that an atom isn't quite like that, but Rutherford was very close, and because of his brilliant work in discovering the cause and nature of radiation, and in working out the structure of atoms, Rutherford is known to this day as the "father of nuclear (atomic) science."

THE ATOMIC AGE

In the eight years from the day when Wilhelm Roentgen discovered X-rays, to the day in 1903 when Rutherford published his explanation of radioactivity, ideas and beliefs that had stood

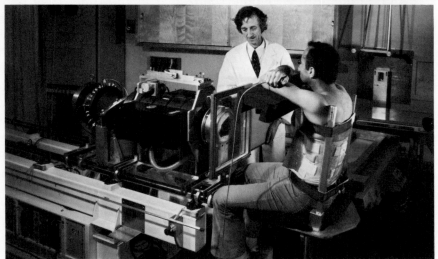

Top left: Uranium mine near Grants, New Mexico.
Top right: Fuel particles of uranium and thorium molded
into finger-sized fuel rods for use in a nuclear reactor.
Above: Radiation therapy for the treatment of cancer.

for hundreds and even thousands of years were swept away. People learned there were invisible rays that could go right through solid objects; that substances which had always been thought to be inactive and "lifeless," were actually actively pouring out such rays; and that the rays were streams of speeding particles from atoms that were tearing themselves apart and changing into something else. People had been given the X-ray, which was one of science's greatest gifts to the fight against disease and injury, and they had been given radium, which turned out to be a powerful weapon against the dreaded disease cancer. Pierre Curie, working with several doctors, had found that radium rays could burn away cancer cells in a person's body, and that the burns would heal, leaving healthy, disease-free cells.

And, although few people realized it at the time, they had also been given a better understanding of the laws and forces that control the entire universe. Now, for the first time in all history, people could begin to understand such things as how the sun works, for it is the activity and motion of the sun's atoms tearing themselves apart that radiates out the heat and light that make life on earth possible.

There were others beside Roentgen, Becquerel, the Curies, and Rutherford and Soddy, who made discoveries and did work that contributed to the final understanding of radioactivity and atoms. In 1899, the year after the Curies made their discoveries of polonium and radium, a French chemist, Andre Debierne, discovered the radioactive metal element *actinium*, and a German, Frederich Ernst Dorn, discovered the radioactive gas element, *radon*. In 1900, Paul Villard, a French physicist, found there was a third kind of radiation beside Alpha and Beta rays, which he named *Gamma rays*, after the third letter of the Greek alphabet. No scientific discovery ever stands entirely on its own; it is always based on a discovery that came before it. The discoveries of Becquerel, the Curies, and these other scientists were all linked together. Most of these people knew one another, and

Two of the greatest minds of science, Marie Curie and
Albert Einstein, are shown together in this rare photograph,
probably taken in 1929 in the United States.

some even worked together at times. Becquerel helped the Curies on occasion, and Pierre Curie and Andre Debierne often talked and worked out problems together. Ernest Rutherford had worked with Joseph Thomson before going to Canada, and Rutherford later often visited the Curies and talked with them. It is almost certain that things these people talked about to one another helped them make the discoveries and do the things they did.

All those discoveries helped to build the kind of world we now live in—a world of atomic power plants, atomic weapons, atomic clocks, atomic submarines, radiation treatments for disease, radioactive dating of rocks and fossils, and many other things that are based on a knowledge of radioactivity. But it was basically the discovery of radium by the Curies that took the science of physics off the plodding path it was following—and which most nineteenth-century physicists felt led to a dead end —and put it on a road that leads to a future we can only guess at!

FURTHER READING

Asimov, Isaac. *How Did We Find Out About Nuclear Power?* New York: Walker, 1976.

Esterer, Arnulf. *Discoverer of X Ray: Wilhelm Conrad Röntgen.* New York: Messner, 1969.

Fermi, Laura. *The Story of Atomic Energy.* New York: Random House, 1961.

Gallant, Roy A. *Explorers of the Atom.* New York: Doubleday, 1974.

Greene, Carol. *Marie Curie, Pioneer Physicist.* Chicago: Children's Press, 1984.

Grey, Vivian. *Secret of the Mysterious Rays: The Discovery of Nuclear Energy.* New York: Basic Books, 1966.

Keller, Mollie. *Marie Curie.* New York: Franklin Watts, 1982.

Kohn, Bernice. *The Peaceful Atom.* Englewood Cliffs, N.J.: Prentice-Hall, 1963.

Lapp, Ralph. *Roads to Discovery*. New York: Harper & Row, 1960.

McKown, Robin. *Giant of the Atom: Ernest Rutherford*. New York: Messner, 1969.

Moche, Dinah. *Radiation: Benefits/Dangers*. New York: Franklin Watts, 1979.

Pringle, Lawrence. *Radiation: Waves and Particles/Benefits and Risks*. Hillside, N.J.: Enslow Publishers, 1983.

Snow, C. P. *The Physicists: A Generation That Changed the World*. Boston: Little, Brown, 1981.

Stepp, Ann. *The Story of Radioactivity*. New York: Harvey House, 1971.

Thorne, Alice. *The Story of Madame Curie*. New York: Grosset & Dunlop, 1959.

INDEX

THE AUTHOR

Tom McGowen is the author of many books in the sciences, including *Album of Dinosaurs*, a Junior Book of the Month Club selection; *Album of Whales*, cited by the National Science Teachers Association as an Outstanding Science Book for Children; and *Album of Prehistoric Man*, selected as a notable book by the National Council for the Social Studies. He has also written fantasy novels and picture books, and in his position as senior editor at World Book, he writes the special *Childcraft* annual.

Mr. McGowen, who is married and lives in Norridge, Illinois, has four children and nine grandchildren.